19.99

GREAT WHITE SHARK

SHARK

MYTH AND REALITY

This work is dedicated to Marine and Evan, Natacha and Milena, with the hope that one day they will have the opportunity to discover the great white shark in domains other than these pages.

A FIREFLY BOOK

Published by Firefly Books Ltd. 2012

First printing

Publisher Cataloging-in-Publication Data (U.S.)

Civard-Racinais, Alexandrine.
Great white shark : myth and reality / Alexandrine Civard-Racinais ; Patrice Héraud.
[144] p. : col. ill., col. maps ; cm.
Includes: bibliographical references and index.
Summary: This title follows one research team as it tracks tagged great whites, revealing previously unknown behaviors such as hunting in groups, changing our understanding of this remarkable animal. It also surveys the deadly dangers faced by great white sharks, such as finning and ocean garbage.
ISBN-13: 978-1-77085-102-3 (pbk.)
1. White shark. I. Héraud, Patrice. II. Title.
597.33 dc23   QL638.95.L3.C4832012

Library and Archives Canada Cataloguing in Publication

A CIP record for this book is available from Library and Archives Canada

Published in the United States by
Firefly Books (U.S.) Inc.
P.O. Box 1338, Ellicott Station
Buffalo, New York 14205

Published in Canada by
Firefly Books Ltd.
66 Leek Crescent
Richmond Hill, Ontario L4B 1H1

English translation: Klaus and Margaret Brausch

Printed in China

This title was developed by Éditions Glénat
BP 177,F – 38008 Grenoble Cedex

Title of the original French Edition: *Le grand requin blanc, du myth à la réalité*
© Éditions Glénat 2011

GREAT WHITE SHARK

MYTH AND REALITY

PHOTOGRAPHS Patrice Héraud
TEXT Alexandrine Civard-Racinais

FIREFLY BOOKS

FOREWORD

Up to 20 feet (6 m) long and with enormous jaws, the great white shark has such a bad reputation as a man eater that it's enough to make your skin crawl! I, along with many others, belong to the generation greatly affected by Steven Spielberg's classic movie *Jaws*. After that, it's been difficult to appreciate the fact that this shark does not systematically seek out humans bobbing on the water's surface. Changing that negative perception is as difficult as swimming against the current. I know a bit about that... Nevertheless, men and women worldwide are working hard to change that perception and provide us with a more enlightened view of these animals. Among these is Dr. Samuel Gruber, an authority on sharks: "Unlike the dolphin's famous smile and the panda's great sad eyes, the shark has nothing like that, only a nasty reputation." The assurance and passion of this 73-year-old man and his knowledge of sharks helped me to overcome my own fears. Thanks to him, I undertook a night dive in the waters off the Bahamas and approached a 13-foot (4 m) tiger shark. I still tremble at the memory and I am not about to repeat that experience. It was dark and I had but one reaction: to get back into the boat as quickly as possible. In hindsight, when I relive the scene, I realize that at no time was I in danger. This impressive shark, which could have made a short meal of us, never exhibited any aggressive behavior toward us. That was to be my first lesson.

My second and most important lesson was based on three words: "We need it." That is, we need to regulate fish populations. Sharks are of great ecological importance, and we need to protect them from overfishing, which is catastrophic for the ecosystem. The oceans are a whole system, wherein each species helps maintain the equilibrium of others. I am most concerned about preserving the oceans and all of their creatures, without distinction or bias. In our eyes, the great white shark is not particularly likeable, and it therefore requires stronger advocacy than more likeable species. This book by Alexandrine Civard-Racinais and Patrice Héraud contributes to this much-needed advocacy for rehabilitation. The bulk of the superb images obtained by Patrice Héraud were taken in open waters, outside protective cages. This does not represent an act of bravery but a reflective attitude and a growing understanding of the great white's behavior. In both words and images, the authors clearly show that it is possible to swim against the currents of shark prejudice.

MAUD FONTENOY

Spokesperson for UNESCO and World Oceans Management, vice president of the Conservatoire National du Littoral, member of the Conseil Économique, Social et Environmental and a devoted sailor. For several years, Maud Fontenoy has been on the forefront of providing public information about worldwide issues related to protection of the seas.

"ANIMALS ARE IN THE SAME SITUATION AS WE ARE...
ENDANGERED SPECIES ON AN ENDANGERED PLANET."
JEFFREY MOUSSAIEFF MASON, *WHEN ELEPHANTS CRY*, 1997

Although some 500 species of sharks populate the oceans, there is one that captures human imagination more than any other, whether in terror or in fascination: the great white.

It is often pictured as a terrifying and bloodthirsty monster. It is certainly fascinating. We fear it because we don't know it (at least not well). For instance it was not until 1965 that an American television crew filmed it for the first time under water! But the goal of filming it is not to make sharks more likable in our eyes but to show them for what they are: powerful and wild predators that one has to respect. We often fear what we don't know and respect more what we understand. Unfortunately we still know very little about the great white shark and have a long way to go before understanding its traits and its behavior.

As our world continues to turn from paradise to garbage dump, all of us who are concerned have two powerful options: protect what we still can or turn a blind eye to progressive extinction. Today the great white is being hunted excessively for its fins, teeth and skin. By what right and in whose name is this happening?

I often hear it said that our efforts to stem humanity's destructive follies are futile, that it is too late to stop this wave of devastation and that it will inexorably affect our forests and oceans and forever sweep away our flora and fauna.

Every day species disappear amid large-scale indifference. Everyone is aware of this, but only a few are trying to reverse this trend. I am proud to count myself among those who fight so that our children and grandchildren can continue to discover those monarchs of the sea in their natural settings rather than in books or museums.

My efforts may be little more than the proverbial drop in the ocean, but I also know that many other drops will join mine in this struggle, namely the preservation of life.

Patrice Héraud

WORLDWIDE DISTRIBUTION OF THE GREAT WHITE SHARK

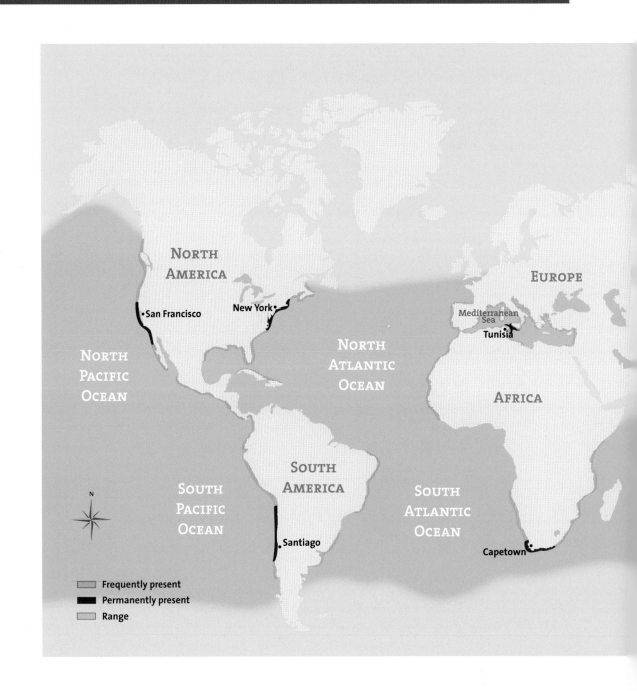

NORTH
AMERICA

EUROPE

•San Francisco

New York•

Mediterranean
Sea

Tunisia

NORTH
PACIFIC
OCEAN

NORTH
ATLANTIC
OCEAN

AFRICA

SOUTH
AMERICA

N

SOUTH
PACIFIC
OCEAN

SOUTH
ATLANTIC
OCEAN

•Santiago

Capetown•

◻ Frequently present
◼ Permanently present
◻ Range

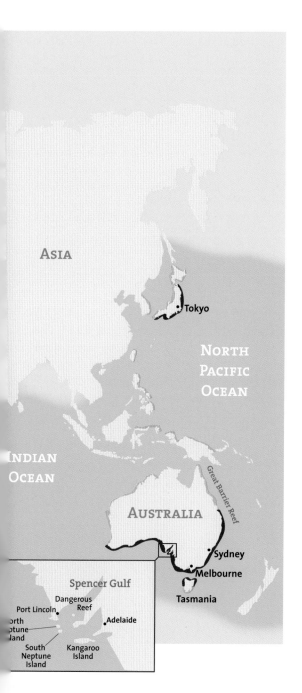

Common name: Great white shark

Scientific name: *Carcharodon carcharias*

Class: Chondrichthyes (this class includes all cartilaginous fish, including rays and sharks)

Order: Lamniformes

Family: Laminidae

Length: 13 to 20 feet (4–6 m) for adults

Weight: 1,500–2,200 pounds (680–1,000 kg) for males; 2,200–4,200 pounds (1,000–1,900 kg) for females; maximum weight can exceed 3 tons.

Longevity: 40–50 years

Speed: Cruising speed 2 miles per hour (3.25 km/h) minimum; can reach up to 30 miles per hour (50 km/h) for brief spurts.

Diet: The great white shark is at the top of the food chain; as an adult (longer than 10 feet/3 m), its principal prey includes seals, sea otters and sea lions. Occasionally it will feed on sea birds, dolphins and other sharks, as well as scavenge (principally on whale carcasses). Juveniles feed preferentially on fish, rays and other sharks.

Active period: daytime

Lifestyle: Mainly solitary but occasionally lives in small groups. A social hierarchy exists based on length, with the longest being dominant.

Reproduction: Females are oviparous (though eggs develop within the genital canal), and individuals deposit from one to 10 fully formed young.

Geographic distribution: As shown in the map, great whites are found in all oceans and seas of the world; they reside in the upper regions of the ocean waters, between 0 and 820 feet (250 m) in depth.

1

PORTRAIT OF
THE GREAT WHITE

*"IT REACHES A VERY GREAT SIZE.
IT HAS BEEN REPORTED THAT
THE STOMACH OF ONE OF THESE
MONSTERS CONTAINED AN ENTIRE
HUMAN BODY, WHICH IS NOT
BEYOND BELIEF CONSIDERING
ITS GREAT PENCHANT FOR HUMAN
FLESH."*

THOMAS PENNANT,
BRITISH ZOOLOGY, 1812.

The great white has been given almost mythical attributes,

since much about it is still a mystery. It has been studied mainly in captivity, and since it is very difficult to observe it in its natural environment, scientists have had to make many assumptions and extrapolations about this shark. No one, for example, really knows the worldwide size of its population. Similarly, major chapters of its life history have yet to be written. Where and how do great white sharks mate? Why do both males and females undertake long oceanic migrations? What is the exact length of their gestation period? How long can they live? While there are still more questions than answers, there is nevertheless constant progress toward understanding these magnificent predators, so perfectly adapted to their environment and endowed by nature and with such remarkable attributes.

ABOVE

The great white shark cruises all of the world's oceans.

OPPOSITE

Open water species like the great white shark have developed body coloration that makes it difficult for prey to detect them.

EFFICIENT CAMOUFLAGE

Sometimes nicknamed "white death," the great white appears white only on its ventral side, while the dorsal portions range from blue-gray to gray-brown. This shrewd camouflage is intended to fool its prey or at least lower its vigilance. Seen from above, its dark dorsal coloration blends with the darkness of the ocean depth, while seen from below, it blends in with surface waters lit by the sun.

The shark's nickname also comes from the fact that it occasionally turns on its back to seize prey, thereby exposing its white underbelly. This inverted approach, however, which was first thought to be common, is actually quite rare.

This type of inverted attack, whereby the shark turns on its back and shows its white underbelly, earned the great white the nickname "white death."

A CARTILAGINOUS SKELETON

We have all seen the skeletons of common food fish, which is made of bone. The majority of fish have this type of bony skeleton, which is partitioned into ridged scales that extend from numerous vertebrae. These ridges constitute their internal skeleton, while their external body scales form the animal's exoskeleton. These fish are known as bony fish and are part of the class Osteichthyes, which includes sharks, rays and chimaeras (a strange type of deep water fish with pectoral fins resembling wings and with a very narrow tail), and they are all in the class Chondrichthyes (from the Greek *khondros* for cartilage), so named because of their cartilaginous skeletons. Light and highly flexible, this type of skeleton accounts for the extraordinary water mobility of sharks in general and the great whites in particular.

A BODY DESIGNED FOR SPEED

Taking all species of shark into account, and considering the average speed for great whites, which is about 2 miles per hour (3.25 km/h), the provisional speed record is held by a shark named Nicole that went on an incredible journey (see page 88) at an average speed of 3 miles per hour (5 km/h). Furthermore, when chasing prey, the great white is capable of bursts of up to 30 miles per hour (50 km/h). This kind of power is provided by two bands of cylindrical muscles on each side of the animal's body. Running from head to tail, these two bands act like pistons and drive the powerful caudal fin. The lateral motion of the tail provides efficient propulsion, causing the animal to swim in its familiar undulating manner.

The caudal fins of sharks propel them through water, while the pectoral fins are used for navigation.

Since the great white uses its tail and caudal fins for propulsion, its two dorsal fins act as stabilizers, while the pectoral fins act as a form of rudder.

Research on shark skin has also helped show how it aids in swimming. The skin is covered with toothlike dermal denticles similar to our own teeth, with pulp, dentine and enamel. Just like teeth, these scales are innervated and supplied with blood and are regularly replaced. They help protect the animal (they provide females with a type of body armor against attacks by males) and reduce water resistance, thereby facilitating a smooth, laminar flow over the entire body.

One of the secrets that allow sharks to swim rapidly and change course without slowing down was revealed in November 2010. According to Amy Lang, a researcher at the University of Alabama, such maneuvers are possible due to the presence of extremely flexible scales that regulate the water's circulatory flow. These structures are located where they are most likely to affect the flow of water, namely behind the gills, along the sides of the body. According to Lang, these structures act in water the same way as the small indentations on the surface of golf balls, which render them more aerodynamic and let them travel further than a smooth ball.

ABOVE

Sharks breathe via the constant flow of water through the gills, which oxygenates the gills and then leaves through the gill slits. Like all members of the class Laminiformes, the great white shark has five pairs of gills.

OPPOSITE

In spite of being covered by protective dermal denticles, females are often injured by males which try to immobilize them during mating by biting their pectoral fin or their neck.

FOLLOWING PAGES

Males are equipped with two reproductive organs, called clasps, which are visible behind their two pelvic fins.

The ultimate final stage of a great white's attack on a seal.

NON FLUCTUAT NEC MERGITUR: IT DOES NOT FLOAT NOR DOES IT SINK

Unlike bony fish, sharks do not have a swim bladder, an organ that helps the animal stay afloat effortlessly. Several adaptations, however, allow them to compensate for this. First, shark skeletons are only half as dense as those of bony fish. In addition, shark livers contain a special oil, called squalene that is six times lighter than sea water. This oil allows sharks to adjust their buoyancy and move rapidly up and down without expending much energy. The liver can amount to 25% of the weight of a great white; for example, the liver could weigh 1,380 pounds (625 kg) in a fish weighing 2.5 tons. In comparison, the liver of an adult man weighs less than 3 pounds (1.3 kg). With such an enormous liver to transform food into energy, the great white is well adapted for long periods of fasting. Because its hunting efforts are often unsuccessful, the great white is not guaranteed three square meals a day.

The great white's two large pectoral fins function much like aircraft wings. They keep the shark's body horizontal and prevent it from falling. These fins can also tilt acting like brakes.

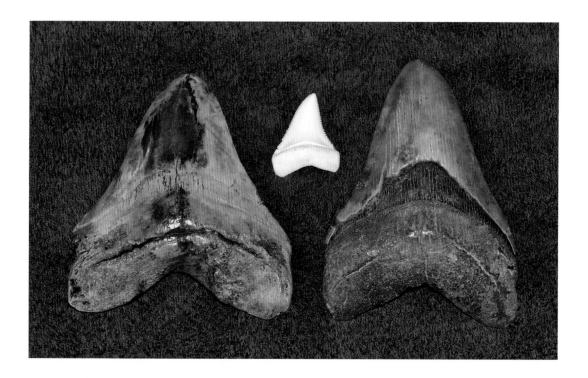

"GREAT WHITE, WHAT BIG TEETH YOU HAVE!"

The 1975 movie *Jaws* reached a wide audience. Indeed, it led some to compare the great white shark to simply a powerful body that propels a pair of no less formidable jaws.

Among other things, shark teeth have the unusual characteristic of not being attached to the skull but linked to it via a series of stretchy ligaments, which gives the animal a remarkable degree of flexibility. At the moment of attack the jaws are extended forward so that they are no longer under the head but in front of it! The great white's jaws open up to 150 degrees, compared to the human's 45 degrees, and it rarely loses its grip on its prey.

During the last stage of an attack, its snout retracts, revealing a highly vascularized upper gum line and most impressive dentition! Directly implanted into the gums, the great white's teeth are constantly replaced by additional layers of new teeth that sit right behind the functioning layer. If one of the frontal teeth is broken or falls off naturally, another tooth advances to take its place. Unique among vertebrates, this system of tooth replacement is common among shark species, thereby permitting them to profit from all feeding opportunities.

Scientists estimate that the great white's mouth holds up to 300 teeth at varying stages of development. A single bite involves about 24 teeth — more than necessary considering they're — up to 3 inches (7.5

ABOVE

A tooth from a 15-foot (4.5 m) great white is shown between two fossilized teeth of a megalodon shark.

BELOW

The shape of a great white's teeth changes with age. Mainly pointed in juveniles, they become triangular, coated and lightly serrated in adults (as shown here).

cm) long — and their efficiency. When the jaws close down again on prey, the upper and lower teeth mesh with each other, forming a deadly trap. At that point the pressure exerted is at least 23 tons per sq. inch (3 metric tons/cm^2). In comparison, *Homo sapiens* only 1.7 tons per sq. inch (220 kg/cm^2). Thanks to its unique musculature, the great white can bite with great force no matter the positioning of its jaws.

Great whites also have to be very solid. Indeed, a team of Australian researchers led by Toni Ferrara (University of New South Wales) discovered that juvenile great white sharks are physically incapable of seizing large prey because their jaws are too fragile. Sharks less than 16 feet (5 m) in length (about 10 years old) can be viewed as awkward teenagers because they are not yet fully grown. In an article published in December 2010 in the *Journal of Biomechanics* scientists reported the results of a study, based on 3-D modeling, that showed the jaws of the great white are reinforced by several layers of mineralized cartilage that take several years to build up. Hence, great whites are not super predators at birth; it takes many years for them to develop that potential.

The shape of the teeth also changes with age. They are pointed in young sharks, which feed primarily on fish, and then become triangular,

SOPHISTICATED SENSORY ORGANS

In order to survive, the great white is equipped with a battery of high-performance senses. For instance, it can detect sound vibrations from an otter at a distance of 1.25 miles (2 km), catch its scent from 330 feet (100 m) and see it dive from several yards away!

Sound vibrations from potential prey are detected through a line running along the shark's flank from head to tail. This "lateral line" consists of a series of small channels containing sensory cells. Filled with a gelatinous substance, these channels perceive the outside world through a series of pores. This allows a shark to detect changes in water displacement and, as a result, the movement of other animals or objects it encounters. This ability has been called "touching at a distance." One can suppose that this creates a sensation halfway between touch and hearing. Sharks also have internal ears, located in two hollows in the skull. These are connected to the exterior via tubular canals that open through a pair of pores on the surface of the skin.

The great white shark's sense of smell is particularly well developed. Located on the sides of its snout, the nostrils can actually detect a single molecule of blood diluted in the equivalent of an Olympic-size swimming pool (one part blood per million parts of water), and they can also transmit that information to the olfactory lobes in its brain. This aptitude to recognize different chemical compounds (in scientific terms, chemoreception) helps not only in seeking prey but also in finding a potential mating partner (because of pheromones emitted during reproductive cycles) and helps the shark detect differences in the salinity of the water in which it is swimming.

These vast marine plains serve as playgrounds for seals and sea otters as well as hunting grounds for the great white, which can hear them from quite a distance.

ABOVE

The great white's highly developed sense of smell lets it detect minute quantities of blood in the water.

LEFT

Tuna form a major part of the great white's diet. Juveniles are particularly fond of it.

Contrary to a now largely discredited notion, the great white has excellent vision, similar to that of higher vertebrates. In addition, nature has endowed it with another clever mechanism: like a cat, great whites have a reflective plaque deep within the retina, the tapetum lucidum, which amplifies the light unto the retina. This provides the shark with better night vision in deep or turbulent waters. In addition, the great white is the only fish that can raise its head above the water to observe its surroundings, much like a submarine uses its periscope.

Some researchers, like marine biologist Ramón Bonfil, have even hypothesized that great whites are capable of celestial navigation, particularly using the positions of the sun and moon, to guide them on their long trans-oceanic migrations. Clearly then, vision is an important sense for great whites, which take great care protecting their eyes. Seals, sea otters and elephant seals are rarely captured without a fight. The risk of eye injury for the shark is consequently very real. In order to avoid damage that would greatly compromise its survival, the great white can completely withdraw its eyes into its eye sockets. Hence, it is temporarily blind during the last few seconds of an attack.

However dangerous such an attack might be, it does not always end tragically for the prey. The great white is actually less voracious than public opinion would have it. Thanks to the presence of sensory pores spread over its skin, the great white often prefers to just bump into potential prey in order to get a "taste" of it. This way, if the prey is not nutritious enough, particularly in terms of fat content, it avoids it. In addition, the shark's mouth and pharynx are lined with papillae and taste buds. That probably explains why a surfer mistaken for prey may be released after an exploratory bite, though with disastrous consequences for the human prey. In addition to the five basic senses of hearing, touch, smell, vision and taste, sharks (along with rays and chimeras) also have a kind of sixth sense unique in the animal kingdom. They are equipped with electroreceptors sensitive to the weak electric field that emanate from every living being. Called "the ampullae of Lorenzini" after the Italian anatomist who first described them in 1678, these receptors are small vesicles covered with sensory cells.

These cells communicate with the exterior via small canals that are exposed to the surface through skin pores, making the snout of the great white shark literally like its nose.

Thanks to the ampullae of Lorenzini, sharks can locate hidden prey through the blinking of an eye or the slightest breathing motion. In addition, these sensors permit sharks to detect variations in their own electrical field. Because of that, scientists think that sharks can also orient themselves with respect to the earth's electromagnetic field. Indirect

During the final stages of an attack, the great white shark retracts its eyes into their sockets in order to better protect them, thereby rendering it momentarily blind.

proof for this supposition was provided in 2004 through satellite tracking of the great white shark Nicole. During the course of her long voyage
(see page 88), this female shark spent 18% of her time at a depth between
1,640 and 2,460 feet (500 – 750 m) with occasional dives down to
3,215 feet (980 m). One theory proposed by researchers is that she gauged
the ocean's depth in order to adjust her direction. It's possible, therefore,
that during the course of their migration, great whites use sight when
they surface but use other senses when diving.

The small dark spots that cover the
head and muzzle are pores. These
pores are connected to the "ampullae
of Lorenzini," which allows the
great white to detect low frequency
electromagnetic fields.

RIGHT

The graceful ballet of an Australian
sea lion.

FOLLOWING PAGES

Sea otters and elephant seals are not
always willing to be meals for the
great white shark, as evidenced by the
many scars visible on the head and
snout of this one.

A FISH THAT DOESN'T LAY EGGS

Unlike female bony fish, the great white shark does not lay eggs. She is oviparous, meaning her eggs form, are fertilized and grow in her genital cavity. This was not known until the 1980s, and scientists are still unsure about the exact gestation time in great whites, which could be as long as 18 months. During this time, the multiple embryos don't exactly live in harmony. Once their source of nourishment (the vitelline sac) is used up, the strongest embryos won't hesitate to feed on unfertilized eggs, a process called oophagy, and some researchers think that the weakest embryos might also be eaten, a process termed "intrauterine cannibalism."

When the time comes, the female delivers one to 10 offspring, which are ready to face the vast ocean and its dangers. As they are born into the ocean, "baby" great whites are already 4–5 feet (1.2–1.5 m) long and weigh 26–33 pounds (12–15 kg). They grow by about 1 foot (30 cm) per year, until males reach about 11$\frac{1}{2}$–12$\frac{1}{2}$ feet (3.5–3.8 m) and females about 15–16$\frac{1}{2}$ feet (4.5–5 m), and they are then capable of reproduction.

Misconception	What we know today
1 There are no great white sharks in the Mediterranean Sea	Great whites are present in all the oceans of the world but also in many other large bodies of water, including the Mediterranean Sea where it resides permanently. In April 2011, a 10-foot (3 m) long great white was captured in international waters between Tunisia and Libya by a Tunisian fishing crew.
2 The great white is only present in tropical waters.	Great whites prefer temperate and sub tropical waters, and while they also visit the tropics, they tend to stay in deeper waters there.
3 The great white is sedentary.	Great whites don't stay in the same location year round. They travel within their territory and also undertake long transoceanic migrations.
4 The great white is the largest of all sharks.	The great white pales in comparison to basking and whale sharks, which can measure 43 and 60 feet (13 and 18 m), respectively.
5 The great white is the most dangerous shark.	All sharks over 6 feet (2 m) are potentially dangerous to humans. Of the 500 species of shark, about 30 fall into this group, including tiger, bull, oceanic white tip and great white sharks.
6 The great white is a stupid brute.	The brain to body weight ratio of sharks falls above that of birds and bony fish. The great white is not a stupid creature but a fish with an evolved brain. Moreover, recent studies by marine biologists indicate behavior more complex than just innate. Some researchers, like Rocky Strong, a biologist at the University of California, Santa Barbara, think that the great whites of South Africa are capable of learning.

Misconception	What we know today
7 The great white is a man-eater.	The International Shark Attack File (ISAF) states that most attacks on humans attributed to great whites are not fatal. In addition, most "attacks" are on objects (boats, surfboards, bodyboards). If humans were really on the great white's menu, they would not stand a chance of escaping. In fact, the great white is not particularly attracted to human blood. Lab tests with smaller species have shown that a sample of human blood elicited a far weaker response than squid or shrimp blood.
8 The great white devours everything in its vicinity.	The great white is very selective in its choice of food. Juveniles are not large enough to consume large prey, whose tough skin and hard bones are too much for their fragile jaws. They must reach adulthood before adding seals, sea otters and elephant seals to their diet.
9 The great white shark is solitary.	Although not yet well understood, the social behavior of great whites is nevertheless far more complex than was previously thought. Groups of great whites have been observed, for example, near Farallon Island, off the coast of California. Marine biologist Mauricio Hoyos thinks that groups of great whites assemble close to Guadalupe Island, Mexico to hunt elephant seals together.
10 The great white shark has no enemies.	Although orcas (killer whales) and larger sharks may on occasion attack smaller great whites, humans are its main predator. The great majority of encounters between humans and sharks end badly — for the shark.

CATHERINE VADON'S PERSPECTIVE

"We must show proof of much curiosity and humility."

No other predator, such as lions or tigers, share such an awful reputation. Why are sharks accused of all sorts of evils? We must look at the writings of the first missionaries and explorers of the 17th century, who returned from tropical areas with the perception that sharks are bloodthirsty creatures. Father Labat who visited the Antilles, readily labeled sharks as demons. His writings definitely had a strong impact on the imagination of Europeans. Let's not forget that "requiem" was the name given by ancient voyagers to *Squalus carchari* (the first name scientific name of the great white), implying that a swimmer who encountered one had no hope but a requiem. An altered version of this word became the French name for shark, "requin."

Within our imperialist environmental culture—our quest to domesticate nature to better dominate and conquer it—the shark is considered a pest to overcome and suppress. The great white shark gets in the way of our nautical activities, so we kill it. Its jaws with terrifying teeth become sought-after trophies, so we kill it. It's essential to understand how the shark is perceived in other parts of the globe, especially in the South Pacific. Before the arrival of Christianity, when the culture among islanders was to live symbiotically with nature, the shark was seen as sacred. The shark was venerated and seen as the reincarnation and symbol of ancestors and gods who visited the world of the living. Some people were permitted to capture sharks, but only according to a strict and complex ritual. Such undertakings were done sparingly, however, and hence the population of sharks was not affected. These people also had a very sophisticated understanding of sharks. For example, the phenomenon of catalepsy, or suspended animation, exhibited by sharks and only recently rediscovered, was well known to islanders, who took advantage of it for fishing. In Fiji, fishermen would wait in their dugouts for a shark to arrive. One of them would then glide quietly into the water and begin stroking the shark's snout and belly, which would totally immobilize it, allowing the other fisherman to quickly tie a rope around its tail. Such notions of respect for the animal should give us pause.

We still have so much to learn about sharks. Many of the latest scientific findings about them are not communicated quickly enough to the public. Let's exhibit curiosity and respect toward this animal we understand so poorly, and let's question our notions of superiority. Let's ask ourselves what their role is in nature instead of trying to subject them to our needs. In this world of instant communication, a suitable spokesperson to advance the cause for their defense is needed — a Diane Fossey for sharks, to rehabilitate and shine the spotlight on them.

Catherine Vadon is assistant professor at the Museum of Natural History in Paris, France and curated the 2006 exhibit Sharks, Between Fear and Understanding.

All of these fish are of no interest to this marauding great white shark. Adults seek more substantive prey.

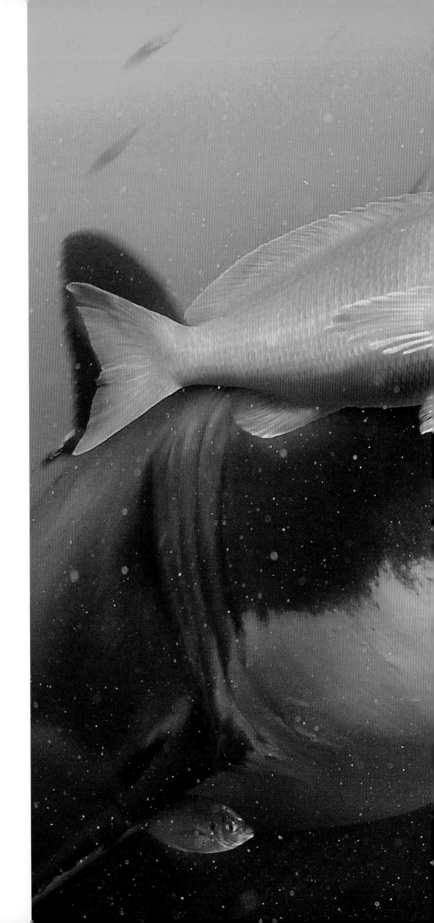

These small fish wait to pick up food scraps after the great white has fed.

2

SEARCHING FOR
THE GREAT WHITE

"AS IF EMERGING FROM A GRAY
MIST ABOUT TWELVE METERS
FROM US, A LEAD-LIKE WHITE
AND GRAY MASS EMERGED, A
TRUE CARCHARODON CARCHARIAS
SOME EIGHT METERS IN LENGTH.
THE MAN-EATING SHARK, AS ALL
EXPERTS AGREED. INSTINCTIVELY
DUMAS AND I CLOSED RANKS. THE
BRUTE ADVANCED SLUGGISHLY...
WHEN THE SHARK SAW US ITS
REACTION WAS THE LAST THING WE
EXPECTED. SEIZED BY TERROR,
THE MONSTER STOPPED, RELEASED
A CLOUD OF EXCREMENT, AND FLED
AT AN INCREDIBLE SPEED."

JACQUES-YVES COUSTEAU,
THE SILENT WORD, 1956

Recounting his first meeting with a great white shark in *The Silent World* (1956), Jacques-Yves Cousteau does not budge from his steadfast rule to represent the great white as a "man-eating shark as all experts agree," a "monster," a "brute" with unpredictable behavior.

Forty-eight years later, when his son Jean-Michel Cousteau wrote *The Great White Shark* to paint a more nuanced portrait of the great white, the younger Cousteau did not forget to underscore that *"Today, my father would describe this meeting quite differently. He was undoubtedly overestimating the size of the animal ... For example, after years of familiarity with the underwater world and its inhabitants, he removed from his vocabulary the words "monster" or "brute" in describing them."*

Our knowledge of the great white has advanced greatly since the late 1950s and since Captain Cousteau's passing. Thanks to tagging programs, conducted since the 2000s by Rodney Fox's Australian foundation (the Fox Shark Research Foundation), our knowledge about the great white has advanced in spectacular fashion during the last two decades.

The results of tracking studies have cast doubt on certain concepts previously thought to be firmly established. Also, further close contact with individual sharks has done much to put to rest the use of words such as "brute" or "monster."

PORT LINCOLN, DOORWAY TO ADVENTURE

"We arrived at Port Lincoln, located 800 kilometers (497 miles) from Adelaide, and base camp for our expedition. The shark cages arrived this morning ... as well as the bait [and] diving and safety gear. Our boat, the Princess II, is being readied for the voyage at sea."
Onboard journal Patrice Héraud, September 9, 2010

We are heading in the direction of the Neptune Islands (North Neptune Island and South Neptune Island), located about five sailing hours from Port Lincoln, in South Australia. These are the last spots of land before the Antarctic, and some of the most favorable for observing great whites.

ABOVE

These tuna are destined as bait for the great white sharks during the process of scientific tagging.

OPPOSITE

The great white sharks being studied by the Fox Shark Research Foundation navigate the waters of the Neptune Islands within a few leagues of Port Lincoln, Australia.

ABOVE

The *Princess II* is the expeditionary vessel of the Fox Shark Research Foundation.

OPPOSITE

Above: Having sailed from Port Lincoln, the *Princess II* arrives near the Neptune Islands, visible here as an outcropping on the horizon.

Below: The sea water basins provide a natural swimming pool for young seals who take their first dives before venturing to the much larger pool.

Sharks cruise year round in these waters where the surface temperature varies between 57–68°F (14–20°C). Adult females are present mostly when the temperatures are between 60.3 and 64.4°F (15.7–18°C), whereas the adult males are mostly observed at temperatures ranging from 57.7 to 64°F (14.3–17.8°C), peaking during the month of September, when water temperatures are at their lowest. The absence of females in springtime and at the beginning of summer is perhaps coincident with their giving birth. They return when the temperatures rise, undoubtedly to provide the young with better development conditions.

The Neptune Islands are also the operational base for the Fox Shark Research Foundation, which has been conducting an extensive tagging program aimed at collecting information about the movements of great whites.

One does not have to search very far to notice the presence of great whites in these waters. Indeed, from the shores of both the South and North Neptune Islands, one can see thousands of black dots. These two islands alone harbor half of New Zealand's population of elephant seals. South Island also represents one of the main reproductive sites of this species. The rare and endangered Australian sea lions are also represented here.

Since the end of 2009, only scientists have been permitted to visit the land masses that encompass the interior of the marine park of the Neptune Islands.

Right

Above: A male fur seal surveys the extent of his domain.

Below: The Neptune Islands consist of rocks and minerals. Vegetation is rare and sparse.

Opposite

Since they are very curious, elephant seals readily pose for the camera, much to the delight of the photographer.

Following Pages

Left: A group of Australian sea lions maraud close to the Neptune Islands.

Right: A young female invites the photographer to play along with her by offering him an abalone shell.

ABOVE

The chum bucket is constantly refilled during the entire expedition. The hose leaving the bucket allows the "appetizing" mixture to make its way into the water.

ABOVE LEFT

As a long, smelly ribbon forms and winds its way behind the boat, the great whites only have to follow its trail.

OPPOSITE

Young elephant seals are easy prey for the great white sharks that patrol not very far from the seal's established colonies.

While elephant seals can be seen on land and in the open sea, sharks are not so easily spotted. Hours can go by, even days, before a team member signals a fin breaking the water's surface or a diver detects the presence of a great white patrolling at 100 feet (30 m) deep. In order to entice sharks to approach the boat, a hose delivers a constant stream of "chum" into the ocean. Carried by wave action, the mixture, consisting of tuna blood and fish flesh and guts, spreads in a dark serpentine fashion, and in no time at all the odor reaches the great whites, however far they may be. All that is left for them to do is to climb this smelly stream to its source.

This large male named Jonny often pops his head out of the water to observe his environment, a behavior unique to these fish.

OPPOSITE

The crew of *Falie* will spend two to three weeks patrolling the Neptune islands.

When, after many hours of waiting, a great white finally displays its dorsal fin, what's left to do is perhaps the most difficult component. We must bring it closer to the foundation's boat in order to proceed with identification and carry out its tagging. To that end, the sight of a good sized tuna generally helps it overcome its shyness. For these purposes, each three-week expedition must carry with it some 1,100 pounds (500 kg) of frozen tuna!

After an extended period, crew members are rewarded a hundred times over when a 14-foot (4.3 m) female named Ufo delights the spectators with amazing leaps. This shark is renowned for her vertical attacks and above-water leaps, each time providing us with a display of unparalleled force and power. Very much like a torpedo, she leaps out from great depths and flings herself on the tuna amid a rolling sea of foam.

This particular kind of attack is rarely observed in Australia. On the other hand, South African great whites off False Bay (which are relatively close genetically to the Australian great whites) have perfected this behavior.

While the great white sharks of False Bay in South Africa habitually make these spectacular leap attacks, this type of behavior is rarely observed among Australian great white sharks. It is even rarer to be able to photograph them in full flight.

South African great whites use this technique very effectively, much to the detriment of this cape's young elephant seals, which colonize Seal Island in numbers up to 65,000 individuals. While at least as fast as the great whites, the elephant seals have greater endurance than their predators, which cannot depend on the element of surprise. Even as the seals try to improve their chances of survival by, for example, taking advantage of early morning hours or dimmer light at dusk, success is not always guaranteed. These kinds of attacks by sharks represent a huge energy investment for animals of their size and weight. They are even putting their lives at risk if two or three such leaps prove unsuccessful.

Even if a great white misses its prey with such a leap, it cannot quit at this point of the chase; if it is to be compensated for the large amount of energy expended it must succeed in catching its prey. The seal, however, has nothing to lose and so mobilizes all of its strength in order to try to escape. If it succeeds in staying out of the shark's grasp long enough, the lord of the seas will often give up the chase.

■ PORTRAIT OF RODNEY FOX

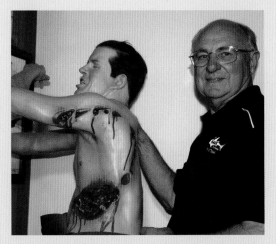

Rodney Fox is a true wonder. His life was turned upside down on December 8, 1963, during an underwater fishing competition half a mile (1 km) off the coast of Australia. While the 23 year-old spear fishing champion was competing, he received a sudden violent punch in the chest, lost his spear and mask, and found himself moving at high speed, trapped "like a bone in a dog's mouth." The dog in question was a great white shark against which Rodney Fox fought with all the energy of a desperate man. Against all odds, luck turned in his favor, but at considerable cost: "The white shark's teeth had dug gaping holes in my chest, baring the contents of my stomach, my lungs and my ribs, almost all of which were broken. The circle of bites spreads up to my left arm, which was slit to the bone." Rodney would require 462 stitches and several months of convalescence to complete his rehabilitation.

Barely up and about, Rodney Fox became obsessed with killing as many sharks as possible, consumed with the idea that "the only good shark is a dead shark." Eventually and thankfully, however, he became aware of the ignorance of such an attitude.

These days, Rodney Fox is one of the world's foremost experts on the great white and one of its greatest defenders: "Despite its size and its exceptional abilities, this shark, with an unjustified reputation, is currently endangered. Will the great white sharks suffer the same fate as the dinosaurs and will we have to be satisfied in the future with photos, replicas of teeth and jaws displayed in museums in order to remember their presence on earth? I hope not!" Seeking to contribute to a better understanding of this "legendary creature," and to initiate protective measures, he founded the Fox Shark Research Foundation (FSRF) in 2002. His son Andrew and researcher Rachel Robbins have joined him in this endeavor.

A SPECIES AND INDIVIDUALS

"Jonny, the featured shark, the crew's mascot, the one that always guarantees a spectacle, finally arrives. He makes a pass and attacks the fish with his jaw wide open above water. When he misses it, he comes close to us, his body bent at a 45° angle. What a showman! He knows what the photographers want of him."
Onboard journal of Patrice Héraud, August 4, 2002

To the uninitiated, one great white shark looks like any other great white shark. Seen side by side, however, they look nothing like each other. Every individual, for example, has a uniquely shaped dorsal fin. Ticka, a young, 11-foot (3.5 m) female, has a dorsal fin that ends in a hook-like shape.

The unique shape of each fin therefore constitutes the first criterion of differentiation. Not unlike a flag swaying in the wind, the delicate posterior portion of a shark's dorsal fin becomes bruised over time, and suffers abrasions following confrontations. For example, the upper portion of Flattop's dorsal fin, a male shark observed in July 2007, has been

Jonny's "smile."

severed and the animal has a bullet embedded in his left flank.

The shape of the dorsal fin, the number and types of notches, clear spots on the lateral fins—these distinguishing marks are to the great white what fingerprints are to human beings. They characterize an individual animal and permit researchers to identify them, along with scars and other markings on the animal's body. In this way, Paillette is readily recognizable through impressive scars visible at the level of her gills. These marks could have resulted from a "love bite" inflicted by a male during rather violent mating (no one has ever filmed the actual mating between two great white sharks, and scientists base their conclusions on observations of mating behavior of other species, such as the nurse shark). Whatever her story, Paillette survived these awful injuries and today measures 15 feet (4.7 m), making her one of the largest individuals we came across in the Neptune Islands.

RIGHT

In order to characterize each shark and be able to recognize it in the future, scientists have several criteria at their disposal, such as clear spots on the body and lateral fins.

OPPOSITE

Above: The shape of the dorsal fin and the markings on the shark's body help in the identification of individual sharks.

Below: This male, named Flattop, is easily recognizable by his dorsal fin, probably sectioned by a boat's propeller.

FOLLOWING PAGES

Bitten by a large male when she was still young, Paillette displays a large scar on her gill slits.

Whether dealing with a satellite or radio transmitter, positioning it on the shark properly requires much patience, a steady aim and an opportune moment. Waiting for that moment can take up to 45 minutes. Once the shark has been located, we must be assured that it meets the right criteria. Finally, we must attract it close enough to the boat with bait in order for the tagging-spear-carrier to carry out his task. Indeed, most tagging done by the Rodney Fox Research Foundation takes place from the diving platform of the *Princess II*.

If a shark refuses to approach the boat or if it displays too much aggression, a cage is lowered. Once inside the cage, the spear-carrier must rely on his guardian angel and tuna carcasses to pique the interest of the predator. This is a dangerous and delicate operation, since the great white is in his element and visibility is often poor.

RIGHT

The Rodney Fox crew is the only one to use the deep-sea cage for its scientific tagging.

OPPOSITE

Hanging from a steel cable, the cage sheltering the divers makes its slow descent into the deep blue sea.

With rare exceptions, visibility is seldom greater than 13–16 feet (4–5 m) in the waters surrounding the Neptune Islands. The photographer took immediate advantage of these clear conditions to photograph the deep-sea cage from above. At 100 feet (30 m) below the surface, on the bottom of the ocean in the waters around the Neptune Islands, this cage allows researchers to approach the most timid of sharks and carry out their tagging.

The diver is responsible for estimating the right time and the proper angle at which to aim the tagging spear so it hits the base of the shark's dorsal fin, solidly implanting the precious transmitter. Without seeming to have felt any pain whatsoever, the shark immediately returns to its routine.

Since the early 2000s, nearly 70 great whites have been tagged in southern Australia by the Fox Shark Research Foundation. In the past few years, the tagging has been preferentially focused on females because of the significant lack of knowledge about the reproduction and gestation period of great whites. To which secret location do the females proceed once they leave the Neptune Islands? To find their way, do they always follow the same course or do they use "alternate itineraries"? Do males and females follow separate courses? Is there an area where males and females converge to mate? Where are the birthing areas?

We hope that upcoming tagging programs will soon provide us with answers to all these questions. Such data on the lifestyle of the great white and its reproductive methods are critical to ensuring the protection and conservation of the species. In addition, the presence of a transmitter might prove to be a deterrent to a poacher.

The deep-sea cage holds four divers. Here, Rodney Fox's son Andrew prepares to tag a shark in open water, a rather delicate operation.

Once the shark is tagged with its transmitter, it is registered in a scientific database that is then forwarded to the Australian Department of Agriculture, Fisheries and Forestry. The shark now bears a name and that, in effect, changes everything. Jean-Michel Cousteau noted the effects of naming at the end of his own expedition in Australia on board the *Alcyone*: "Having seen Foxy, Minus and Mathilda up close, and touched them in a way by tagging them and naming them, they were no longer simply sharks, they were now our sharks and, to our astonishment, this mattered." Since January 2010, Paillette and Biscotto are no longer two sharks among many others. They now matter in the eyes of the children of the Flora-Tristan school at Martignas-sur-Jalle (in Gironde, France), who financed the purchase of the two transmitters and who named the two sharks. Paillette and Biscotto have become goodwill ambassadors of their species, in the same manner as Ticka and Jammie.

This shark was tagged by the Fox Shark Research Foundation. The radio transmitter is permanently implanted, and clearly visible, at the base of its dorsal fin.

Toward what secret destination is
this male heading? Will he be using
the same route as the females or a
different one? These are all questions
the scientific tagging program of the
Fox Shark Research Foundation is
seeking to answer.

It would seem, therefore, that the Neptune Islands constitute an obligatory base for great white sharks during their migration. Thus, the Australian tagging program conducted by the Fox Shark Research Foundation may enable us to determine whether or not the routes traveled by sharks differ in relation to gender, size or season. These studies will also determine how loyal sharks are to certain locations. Each year, sharks tagged from previous expeditions are observed in the vicinity of the Neptune Islands. This is particularly true for Jonny, who has been present every year between the months of May and September since the year 2000. On the other hand, some of his fellow sharks have never returned there. Could it be that they have crossed paths with poachers, trawlers or trophy-seekers, or perhaps they have migrated to other waters? No one knows for sure as yet, but we hope that future expeditions will help clarify these mysteries.

However, recent results confirm once and for all that female sharks tend to undertake very long journeys, some of which rise to the level of incredible feats. Nicole, another female, holds the record for the longest transoceanic migration ever recorded for a great white shark, a return journey of more than 12,400 miles (20,000 km) from the southernmost point of the African continent to the western section of Australia — and all this in less than nine months!

◼ NICOLE'S ODYSSEY

"Nicole went all the way to Australia!" That enthusiastic e-mail, sent by the marine biologist Ramón Bonfil, succeeded in causing his Swiss colleague Michael Scholl to jump for joy.

It all began on November 7, 2003, at Dyer Island in South Africa, after a 12-foot (3.8 m) female, a familiar sight in those parts, was tagged with a satellite transmitter. On February 28, 2004, the transmitter surfaced and began to send signals from a point located 23 miles (37 km) off the northwest coast of Australia. In his New York offices of the Wildlife Conservation Society (WCS), Ramón Bonfil could not believe his eyes when the first results arrived on his computer. Nicole had traveled some 6,835 miles (11,000 km) in the span of only 90 days! Nothing like this had ever been seen before. On her journey, Nicole surpassed all shark distance records, all while swimming at the speed of a cruise ship — about 3 miles per hour (4.7 km/h). This bested the fastest tuna, and she also dove down to 3,215 feet (980 m), a depth never previously recorded.

Nor did her journey end there. On August 20, 2004, Nicole was once again in the vicinity of Dyer Island, where Michael Scholl was able to formally identify her from photographic records. The young female had just concluded a round trip of at least 12,400 miles (20,000 km) between South Africa and Australia. These results, published in the prestigious journal *Science*, cast doubts on what scientists had held as established. The theory was that females were more attached to their birthplace than males, and that only males were capable of undertaking long relocation journeys. The press quickly got wind of this phenomenon.

Less prone to wandering than her celebrated godmother, Nicole (so named by scientists in homage to the Australian actress Nicole Kidman, who is passionate about sharks) dealt well with the sudden media attention. However, Michael Scholl lost all traces of her in November 2004:

> Nicole was a shark very faithful to this region. She would arrive around July and August and would leave again around November – December. I was there up until January 2007. Despite nearly daily expeditions, I never saw her again. We have no idea what happened to her.

Ramon Bonfil, Michael Scholl, et al, "Transoceanic Migration, Spatial Dynamics, and Population Linkages of Great White Sharks," Science 310:100-103, October 7, 2005.

Thanks to Nicole, we now know that female sharks readily undertake very long transoceanic migrations and distance themselves from coastal regions. The motivation for this behavior is not readily apparent. Are they responding to some urgent signal? Do they join up with males, somewhere in the vast ocean, in search of mating partners? Do they leave the reassuring proximity of the islands populated with pinnipeds and the promise of a well-stocked food source in order to give birth in other waters? Also, how do they feed while swimming at great depths? All these questions remain, for the time being, without answers.

However, thanks to Nicole, the need to broaden the protection afforded to great white sharks at close proximity to coastlines has become quite obvious, since such long journeys expose them to numerous dangers and increase their risk of being killed. Ticka, Jammie and Jonny, as well as others, while protected in South Africa and Australia, are not so protected in international waters or along some other coastlines.

Since 2004, the great white shark has been registered in Article II of the Convention on International Trade in Endangered Species of Wild Fauna and Flora (CITES). CITES controls and regulates the international trade in the species it lists. Article II includes all species whose specimen trade must be regulated to avoid exploitation that could threaten their survival. While listing the great white shark in the latest CITES document represents a step forward, this must not be confused with a guaranteed lifeline.

Thanks to more data collection, scientists are beginning to acquire more and more knowledge about this poorly understood animal, whose first images date back to the 1960s.

As night falls on the waters off the Neptune Islands, the time has come for the great white to begin hunting.

3

REQUIEM FOR
THE GREAT WHITE?

"[T]HIS SCOURGE IS NOTHING COMPARED TO WHAT WILL BEFALL OUR ANCESTORS ONCE THE SEAS ARE DEPLETED OF WHALES AND SEALS. AT THAT POINT, CLUTTERED WITH OCTOPI, MEDUSAS AND SQUID, THEY WILL BECOME WASTELANDS OF INFECTION BECAUSE THEIR CURRENTS WILL NO LONGER CARRY THE "HUGE STOMACHS THAT GOD HAS CHARGED WITH SKIMMING THE SURFACE OF THE SEAS."

JULES VERNE, *TWENTY THOUSAND LEAGUES UNDER THE SEA*, 1869

According to many who have called it "white death," the great white is the incarnation of evil. Nevertheless, statistics are hard to ignore. According to the International Shark Attack File (ISAF), between 2000 and 2010, of the 700 reported shark attacks, only 66 were attributed to a great white, with a total of 14 mortalities.

During the same time period, "sports" fishing and commercial exploitation of the seas has reached the point where sharks are at risk of extinction. More than 25% of shark species worldwide are threatened. Taking all species into account, an astonishing 100 million sharks are killed each year. Because of its fragile biology, the great white shark might not make it to the end of the 21st century. This fact has been met with almost universal indifference. The great white is the victim of both mankind's insatiable appetite and the shark's unacceptably inaccurate depiction in the film *Jaws*.

ABOVE

Signs warning the public of the presence of sharks can be found on many Australian beaches.

OPPOSITE

Top: The notion that the great white is nothing but a "killing machine" lusting for human flesh is further contradicted as we learn more about it. The territorial behavior of this female is atypical; most of the time they are mainly curious and placid.

Bottom: Seen from below, a person on a surfboard has a silhouette similar to that of a seal. Pictured here is a surfboard bitten by mistake. The surfer escaped without injury.

GREAT WHITE SHARK ATTACKS: FROM MYTH TO REALITY

Even a cursory search of YouTube gives you an idea of the morbid fascination people have with shark attacks. Searching with the phrase "white sharks attack" brings up thousands of results. These spectacular videos include an attack on an Australian surfer by two great whites (with no more serious outcome than several bite marks on his hand), which attracted up to 6 million international viewers. Some of these online videos are quite graphic and sensationalist.

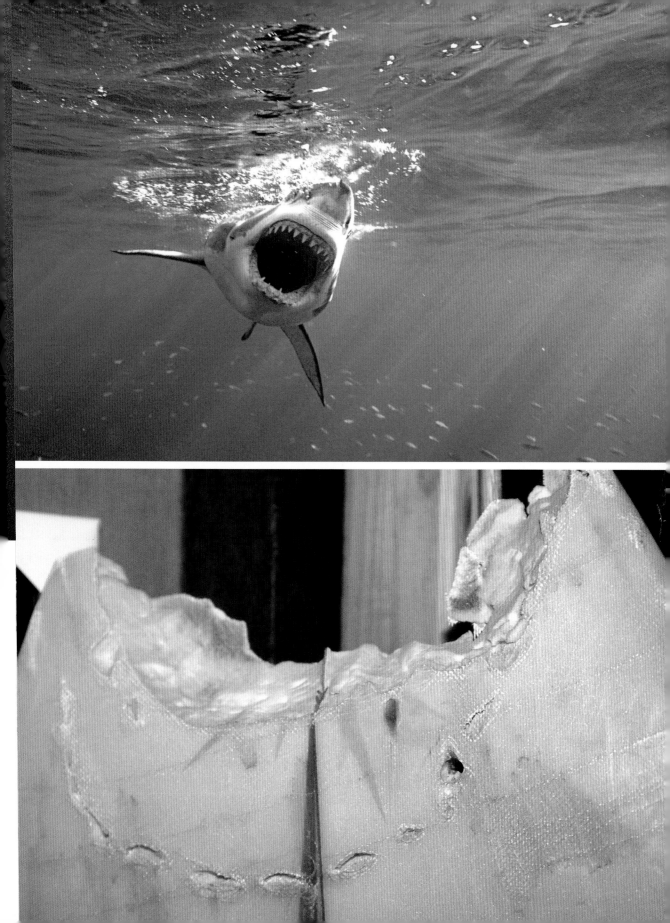

The increase in the number of shark encounters in recent decades is due to the fact that more people have ventured into the seas and oceans. As a result, the frequency of human-shark interaction has risen, and the risk of possible conflict has correspondingly increased as well.

The majority of shark victims are young men. Water sports that attract sharks, including surfing, body-surfing and boogie-boarding, are especially popular among males aged 15–25. Still, these young men are at higher risk of drowning than suddenly finding themselves in a scene from *Jaws*. Sex and age aside, in Australia one shark attack is reported for every 50 drownings, in South Africa one attack is reported for every 600 drownings and in the United States one attack is reported for every 1,000 drownings.

Relative to the world's population as a whole, the probability of dying from a shark attack is insignificant. According to ISAF estimates, such odds were 1 in 3.7 million in 2003. Wasps and snakebites account for far more fatalities than sharks, while malaria-carrying mosquitoes alone cause nearly 800,000 deaths each year.

Outside a cage carrying curious animals dressed in black, great white sharks circulate to investigate and then resume their normal activities.

While a media report of a shark attack has great public impact, it is important to establish what caused it. In cases of so-called "unprovoked" attacks by a great white, several possibilities can be considered. Even if the victim did not intend to be confrontational, it's possible the animal perceived it as such. The attack might then be due to the shark's "social response" to an invasion of its personal space or hunting territory.

Most researchers are convinced, however, that a majority of non-provoked attacks are due to confusion about food, especially near colonies of seals and sea otters. According to George Burgess, director of ISAF, "A human on a surf board or a diver in a dark suit can easily be mistaken for a seal from the depth perspective of a great white shark on the hunt. Since humans are not generally part of their feeding regimen, this can explain such errors." In fact, such reported attacks involve mainly adult sharks longer than 16 feet (5 m), who feed principally on marine mammals, unlike younger sharks, whose jaws are not yet adapted to such prey.

Lacking hands, sharks use their mouths to gain information on any new object.

This shark's behavior is aimed
at intimidating an overly
inquisitive petrel.

The fragility of juvenile shark jaws, according to a 2010 Australian study (see page 26) might also explain why some attacks on humans stop after an initial exploratory bite that is generally not fatal.

This shark is not out to attack the boat and its occupants. It is simply attracted by the electric field emitted by the outboard motor. Propeller blades often inflict serious injury to these animals.

Lacking hands, sharks rely on the papillae and taste buds inside their mouths to identify a new object to which they are attracted, out of curiosity or as potential food. That's why the most curious sharks nibble the bars of diving cages or boat engines without going any further. Are they even aware that they have encountered their top predator?

FRÉDÉRIC BUYLE'S
PERSPECTIVE

"At no time did we feel that we were about to become prey."

I have been diving with great white sharks for several years, specifically off the South African coast, where I have many friends among divers and underwater fishermen who have gotten together many times for hunting trips without any media present. Still, the media continue to focus on sensationalist images. A mean great white devouring anything at all is inevitably more newsworthy than a timid animal.

Pierre Frolla, who dives without breathing equipment, William Winram and I, have done a lot of diving off South Africa. When we announced that we were going to dive with sharks off Guadalupe Island in Mexico, several people told us, "Be careful, you are going to be devoured, the waters are clearer there and the sharks more aggressive." Suddenly we became a little fearful, finding that odd, since a great white shark remains a great white shark; even if their environment is different, they still retain the same feeding habits. On our first day aboard the boat, we noticed that the Mexican great whites moved around in the same manner as the South African sharks. Once in the water, we discovered that they indeed exhibited the same kind of behavior as their fellow creatures, as well as the same differences in size and sex. Adult females are very sure of themselves while juveniles are more hesitant. One of the advantages of this location is that underwater visibility is exceptional. Another advantage is that at this time of year (the end of October and beginning of November) great whites feed almost entirely on elephant seals. Often we found ourselves surrounded by sea otters, but the great whites didn't even look at them. At no time did we feel that we were about to become prey.

Ultimately the Guadalupe sharks proved to be more timid than their South African counterparts. We had to gain their confidence in order to approach them. Most of the notions about this shark are based on the images that have circulated. However, more than 99.9% of these images show great whites maniacally attacking their prey with gaping mouths. When there is little or no prey their behavior is totally different. Like all predators, the great white will not risk attacking a prey it does not know or one that might pose a danger to it. If it misses or its strike fails, it will pay dearly. A diver without breathing equipment will not be passive. He will look at the shark, go towards it or move away to make it come toward him. The shark will know it has been spotted and that it does not have the upper hand. A diver with flippers is about 8 feet (2.5 m) long, almost as long as a typical shark, which is 10 feet (3 m) long. There is also the notion of being proactive. If a diver wants the shark to approach him, he can curl up a bit and stretch out again. If a young male approaches too closely, a diver can stretch out and move toward it, at which point the shark will back away. A social hierarchy exists among sharks, with larger individuals dominating. Dominant sharks are always above the others in the water column.

Since divers are usually above the sharks, which places them in a dominant position, they can take advantage of that. In fact, one often senses a certain confusion among the largest sharks.

Approaching a great white shark in open waters without the safety of a protective cage is a magical experience undertaken by more and more divers.

Most of the accidents that happen involve swimmers, surfers and under water fishermen, who don't see the animals and so cannot behave in a proactive manner toward them. Among intentional provoked encounters, there have never been any accidents. If a shark comes toward you, don't make a hasty retreat, but affirm your position in the water. This will reassure the animal and establish contact with it, but, of course don't ever forget that this is a wild animal.

Frédéric Buyle is an underwater photographer, a free diver (a diver who dives without an air supply) and a former free-diving world champion

MAN—THE GREAT WHITE'S PREDATOR

In 2010 the great white shark was accorded the sad distinction of being listed among the 10 most threatened species by the World Wildlife Fund (WWF). This sounded an alarm to raise public awareness, since the great white is the tree that hides the forest. Sharks, rays and chimeras pay a heavy price for commercial and recreational fishing. Experts from the International Union for the Preservation of Nature (IUPN) estimate that in the north east Atlantic alone, a major fishing area for many European countries, 26% of all Chondrichthyes (including sharks) are in danger. Moreover, 7% of the northeast Atlantic's Chondrichtyes are on the "critical extinction" list, meaning they are likely to disappear in the coming years, 7% are "threatened" and 12% are listed as "vulnerable."

On a worldwide level, of the 1,038 species of Chondrichtyes evaluated by experts from the IUCN, 18% are threatened, of which 3% are listed as critical, 4% in danger and 11% as vulnerable. Based on the Red List of threatened species, the great white shark has been listed as vulnerable since 1996, which means it is at a high risk of extinction in the wild.

Although seen as a symbol of strength, the great white is far more fragile than it appears. Some of its natural attributes actually work against it. While it grows relatively quickly, it does not reach sexual maturity until quite late. Males reach sexual maturity at eight or nine years, when they are between 11½–13 feet (3½–4 m) long. Most females must wait until they are 12 to 14 years old and have attained a size of 13–15 feet (4 – 4½ m) before they are ready to withstand the furious assaults of their mates. Noting the rarity of sexually mature females, the IUCN species safeguarding committee suggests that this is most likely due to females being over-fished before they are reproductively mature.

RIGHT

There is no aggression or violence in this type of behavior. The shark has approached to taste the unknown object and then resumes its underwater ballet.

OPPOSITE

The photographer left his cage to get this photo, without the slightest interest from this pregnant female.

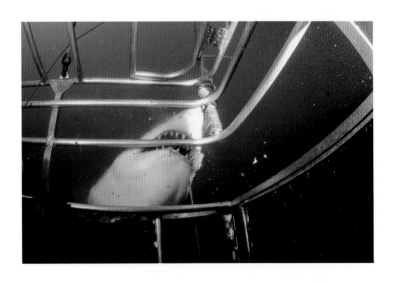

■ PUTTING AN END TO FINNING

"Sharks are like pigs, everything in it is good to eat," summarizes Bernard Séret, a researcher and shark specialist at the Institut de recherche pour le développement (the developmental research institute) of the Muséum national d'histoire naturelle (national museum of natural history/MNHN). Everything tastes good, especially shark fins. Once cleaned and dried, they are used to prepare shark fin soup, which is much prized in many Asian countries, which ascribe curative qualities to it and claim that it is an aphrodisiac.

Demand for fins has risen sharply since the end of the 1980s thanks to the economic growth of Asian countries and the rise of a wealthy middle class in China. Researchers have estimated that that the minimum number of sharks killed each year solely for their fins is 73 million. Species-specific killing on this scale has created a true ecological crisis. In some European fishing areas only 5% of the sharks caught are actually kept, largely due to the great differential between Hong Kong prices — up to $295 per pound ($650/kg) of shark meat — versus $.90 to $4 per pound ($2–9/kg) in European markets. In order to avoid filling vessel cargo holds with larger carcasses of little economic value, the sharks are thrown back into the sea alive, after their fins have been cut off.

This cruel practice, called "finning," has been strongly condemned by the Shark Alliance, a coalition of 110 organizations worldwide. Their goal is to lobby for improved shark conservation, especially among members of the European Union, who are the largest exporters of shark fins to China. The Shark Alliance is specifically lobbying to revise the agreement banning finning that was adopted in 2003. Since that time, cutting shark fins aboard ships has been banned, unless a special permit has been granted. In reality, however, these EU regulations still make finning possible and, for all intents and purposes, uncontrollable.

According to the Shark Alliance, the simplest and most efficient way to end finning would be to unload intact animals in ports (with fins remaining naturally attached to the body). This procedure is actually widely practiced in most Central American counties, as well as in many areas of the United States and Australia. In December 2010, the European parliament concurred with this policy, but the battle is not over.

"The consumption of [shark] fins should be banned," Bernard Séret has angrily declared , adding, "Decimating entire populations of fish for the pleasure of a few wealthy people is an ethical scandal! The agony of sharks whose fins have been cut off can last up to 90 days. If they can no longer swim they cannot breathe. Beyond ethical concerns, throwing carcasses back into the sea creates both an ecological and an economic mess since the meat could still be consumed."

In April 2010, Hawaii became the first American state to pass a law banning the sale, possession and distribution of shark fins. Other American states have since followed suit. However, China, the world's largest importer and consumer of shark meat and fins, must still be convinced.

ABOVE

Dried shark fins for sale in a Hong Kong store.

LEFT

Close to 100 million sharks are massacred each year, the victims of overfishing and a growing demand for their fins.

Great white sharks have actually become "accessory" catches of large commercial fisheries. Trawler boats, bottom nets, long fishing lines with multiple hooks, fish traps, herring barriers and drift nets (nets circling and following fishing vessels at the start of sailing) are, unfortunately, not selective and remain the main cause of death of great whites, even in protected areas like Australia. The dissection of an 18-foot (5.5 m) adult female, caught by Australian fishermen in 2000, found no less than eight large fish hooks and several feet of fishing net in her stomach. On the other hand, the high demand for shark fins is not an incentive for fishermen to return their prize back into the sea even if they are still alive.

In similar fashion, nets intended to protect beaches in southern Australia also wreak havoc among juvenile sharks, that is, those less than 6½ feet (2 m) long, which get entangled and end up drowning. This observation has led researchers to propose that habitats near shorelines might serve as nurseries or points of assembly for juveniles. Such habitats and their fauna are also threatened by increasing human populations

BELOW

The city of Port Lincoln in South Australia has profited considerably from commercial tuna fishing. Raised in huge fish farms, the tuna are an irresistible attraction for the great white shark, which is very abundant in this region.

FOLLOWING DOUBLE PAGE

Intended to catch tuna or swordfish, these nets, 100–130 feet (30–40 m) wide by up to 60 miles (100 km) long, make victims of many great white sharks as collateral damage. Those that don't die from asphyxiation retain the scars of such encounters.

and the resultant pollution. Pesticides, heavy metals and other toxic substances become concentrated in the bodies of these predators at the top of their food chain. Unlike polar bears, which have gained widespread public sympathy, great whites enjoy no such benefits.

Individual sharks that do manage to pass through the mesh of netting become both figuratively and literally the prey of trophy hunters. These people are particularly interested in the largest animals, that is to say, the biggest males and females primed for reproduction, in order to sell their teeth and jaws to tourists. Currently, a very large set of jaws can fetch the incredibly high sum of $65,000 and a single tooth between $650–1,000.

Finally, as mentioned above, females toward the end of gestation can get trapped in protective beach netting , ostensibly as they come close to shore to give birth. IUCN experts have even discovered the existence of a market for newborn sharks.

Even though great whites have been classified as endangered species in an appendix II of CITES (the Convention on International Trade in Endangered Species), since 2004 they can still be fished commercially, meaning their survival is not guaranteed. In some areas of our ocean planet, the situation is already critical. A group of researchers at Stanford University in California published a paper in *Biology Letters* in March 2011 that outlined preliminary estimates of the number of great white sharks off the coast of central California. Only 219 adults and juveniles were counted in that region of the Pacific, a number far lower than scientists expected. They also underscored that this population was "far lower than that of other marine predators like orcas and polar bears," and this in a region naturally and historically frequented by great white.

Another hot-point, Australia, has lost an estimated 60 – 95% of its great white population over the past 50 years. However, these are not official numbers, due to the large seasonal variation within shark populations. At this point in time, it is likely that less than 10 million individual great whites are present in Australian waters, a number that is unfortunately hard to verify.

OPPOSITE

The jaws of great white sharks are in high demand by trophy hunters. Seen here is a reproduction of the jaws of a 16-foot (5 m) animal captured in the Mediterranean Sea.

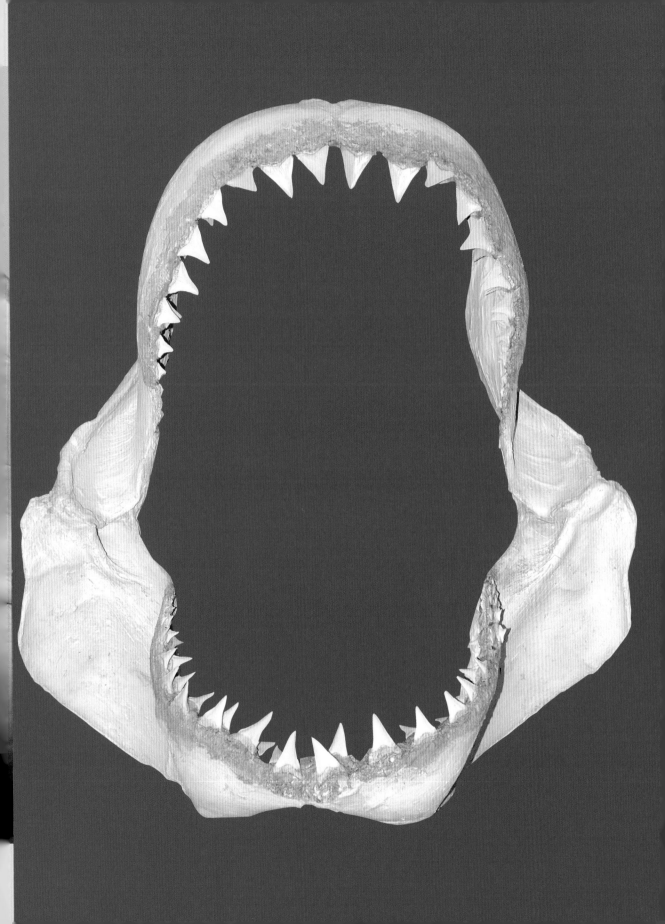

Despite the successful removal of
the plastic strap by members of the
Fox Shark Research Foundation, it is
possible that Strappy did not survive
his deep wounds.

Closer to home, the Committee on the Status of Endangered Wildlife in Canada (COSEWIC) has clearly stated that the great white is disappearing from Canadian waters. Decimated by American long line fishing flotillas operating in the north-west Atlantic, shark populations in the area dropped from 59% to 89% between 1986 and 2000. In 2006, this led the Canadian Ministry of Fisheries and Oceans to estimate: "Any level of damage would result in its demise or disabling its rehabilitation." It is therefore urgent to react to make sure that the great white does not disappear forever from the oceans and in order to avoid even more damage to our fragile marine ecosystems.

RIGHT

Less than 10,000 great white sharks remain in Australian waters.

OPPOSITE

Although mysterious and feared, the great white shark is an evolutionary marvel.

Situated at the top of the food chain, the great white shark plays an essential role in maintaining the good health of marine ecosystems.

ECOTOURISM: IS IT SAVING THE GREAT WHITE?

All attempts to keep great white sharks in captivity have failed. We cannot, therefore, rely on aquatic parks to assure its population is replenished. In 2004, California's Monterey Bay Aquarium surpassed all records in managing to keep a young female for 198 days. After having killed two other sharks living with her in a 10,000-gallon (38,000 L) tank, and having displayed signs of aggression, she was released to the ocean in March 2005. A year and a half later, another attempt was made following the accidental capture of a young male. He remained on display for 137 days before being released as well in January 2007. Before these releases, throngs of visitors were able to view the animals. The small female alone was able to attract close to 1 million people.

Paradoxically, humankind's fascination with the great white shark could lead to a reversal of its fortunes as more and more tourists seem willing to dive into the water to view them in their natural habitat. Because of this trend, perhaps a great white shark will one day be more valuable alive than dead.

As a consequence of the increased popularity of ecotourism, deep-sea cage diving has become a very lucrative business in the past decade. Notably, Gansbaai, a small fishing village 110 miles (180 km) from Cape Town, South Africa, is now considered the worldwide capital for great white observation. Eight boat operators now share the tourist trade. In 2006, about 42,000 tourists partook in surface cage diving in order to observe the great white in its natural habitat.

There is no need to be a seasoned diver for this adventure. Anchored solidly to the boat and kept above water by flotation devices, the metal

cage in which the dives take place is accessible to many people at once. Even the most fearful of visitors can still observe the show from the boat's bridge.

Gansbaai is not the only favorable location for this kind of shark observation. False Bay, Dyer Island and Mossel Bay in South Africa, the Neptune Islands in South Australia, Guadalupe island off Mexico's Pacific coast, as well as the Farallon Islands and Channel Islands near the California coast, are all suitable for this kind of shark viewing.

In the past few years, however, a number of ecological and conservation associations have voiced reservations about such cage diving, maintaining it disturbs the great whites' behavior.

There are indeed serious issues to consider, including the magnetic field of metal cages, the noise of boat engines and the potential danger posed by boat propellers. Another menace is the bait routinely deployed by boat operators to entice the animals. This could, in turn, attract great white sharks closer to pleasure boats and beaches.

In order to further investigate the possible increased risk due to unwanted shark encounters, a study was undertaken by researchers

"Shark! Shark!" The spotter has just seen a great white shark; adrenalin rushes up a notch.

from the University of Hawaii at Manoa. The results, published in July of 2009 in the *Environmental Conservation Journal,* concluded that there is "a negligible impact of caged deep-sea diving on the public's safety." The authors emphasized that no increase in attacks on the north coast of the Island of Hawaii was recorded since the arrival of tour operators (the study was conducted between 2004 and 2008).

Regarding the potential negative impact of cage diving on the great whites' behavior, no definitive conclusions can be drawn one way or another. Charlie Huveneers (SARDI Aquatic Sciences), a specialist in the great whites of southern Australia, has stated that, "Tourism undoubtedly has its effects. However, are these effects always negative? We have yet to arrive at a definitive answer to this question. When the boats are present, we have observed that certain sharks spend more time around them. Is it then more harmful for them to spend time at a specific location instead of swimming around the island? The impact may be negative if the presence of the boats diverts the shark from its favorite quarry or if it stops them from doing what they usually do at this

Cage diving offers the opportunity to observe the great white shark close up without harm. Strong emotions and great happiness are guaranteed.

"Ecotourism can be a formidable tool to promote awareness."

The best way to change the manner in which people perceive the great white is to observe it in its element. To this end, cage dives can be extraordinary tools to promote public awareness as long as tour operators follow the rules and the practice is regulated by public agencies. We are dealing with a wild animal that we need to approach cautiously and respectfully. Unfortunately, to the animal's detriment, such cage dives have become a profitable business. In 1997, when I moved to Gansbaai, there were five tour boats, the largest of which could accommodate a maximum of 10 people. They went out three days a week and were rarely filled to capacity.

Today, there are eight boats, the largest of which can accommodate 40 people, and they go out three to four times a day. Every day, hundreds of tourists eagerly await the possibility of catching sight of a great white. Each tourist pays $80–200. Operators generally plan two-hour tours, but, under normal circumstances, four to six hours are required before the sharks may appear. The rocking boat holds some 30 people, who stomp their feet. When a shark is spotted, the operator quickly lowers five tourists in a large cage, lets the shark catch the bait and pulls it in as close as possible to the cage. When the animal comes into contact with the cage, it panics, bites the crossbars, occasionally wounds itself and panics even more... Sharks that are new to the area heal quickly because of their fresh skin, but animals that have been there for a while are covered in scars. This is unacceptable! Tourists get their money's worth, however, and the preconceived notion that the shark is an aggressive animal is further reinforced. Despite all efforts, this adventure bears no resemblance to the animal's natural behavior.

The shark is essentially a fearful animal. In the presence of a diver in a cage, it will approach cautiously, scope what is involved and leave. We must find another operating model, similar to land safaris, with well-informed guides who take time to explain to tourists what they are about to witness and educate them about protecting their environment. Unfortunately, this is not always the case. A few years ago, while I was onboard one of these boats, the guide asked me if sharks were mammals. I thought he was kidding! These boat operators must become goodwill ambassadors for the great white shark.

Michael Scholl is a teacher and biologist specializing in the great white shark, which he has studied during 10 years spent in South Africa.

Cage diving can be an excellent tool to sensitize and educate the public about sharks, as long as tour operators follow a course of good behavior and adopt a respectful attitude toward these animals.

This is the real face of the great white shark, as it appears most often to divers: a huge fish with a spindle-shaped profile, moving elegantly and emitting an unbelievable sense of power and freedom. Perhaps this is one of the last lords of the sea.

PROTECTION LEGISLATION

Country or region	Protection perimeter	Date
Australia	The great white shark is protected in Commonwealth waters (Environmental Protection Biodiversity Conservation Act). It is also protected in the waters of all the states and territories of Australia (Fisheries Law). It is classified as "vulnerable" (the Law on Endangered Species).	1999 (amended in 2001)
European Union (Atlantic coasts)	It is forbidden to fish for great whites, to possess them on board, to transport them or to remove them.	2006
Honduras	Commercial fishing of the great white shark is forbidden. Worldwide appeal to safeguard sharks (September 2010).	2010
The Maldives	General protection—perimeter unspecified.	2010
Malta	Ratification of the species listing of Annex II from the Barcelona Convention of 1995. Ratification of the Berne Convention on the conservation of wildlife and natural habitats throughout Europe. This convention hopes to confer strict protection of the great white shark and forbids damaging or destroying reproduction sites.	2000
Micronesia	Commercial fishing of the great white shark is forbidden. This small state has rendered its territorial waters and its exclusive economic zones as the very first official sanctuaries to protect sharks.	2009
Namibia	It is forbidden to intentionally kill or to sell a great white shark (Fisheries Law).	1993
New Zealand	The great white shark, whose name was added to the list of species protected by the Wildlife Act (1953), cannot be fished for commercial trade. Accidental capturing can, however, be traded commercially. Limited recreational fishing.	2007
South Africa	It is forbidden to intentionally kill or to sell a great white shark (Fisheries Law).	1991
United States	The great white shark is protected in the waters of California and Florida. Capturing these animals for the purpose of commerce is forbidden along the Atlantic coast and the Gulf of Mexico.	1993 (ratified in 1997)

BOOKS

For juvenile readers

• Musgrave, Ruth. *Everything Sharks: All the Facts, Photos and Fun That You Can Sink Your Teeth Into.* Washington, DC: National Geographic Society, 2011.

• Vadon, Catherine. *Meet the Shark.* Lanham, MD: Cooper Square Publishing/Two-Can Publishing, 2007.

For adult readers

• Bright, Michael. *Sharks.* Buffalo, NY: Firefly Books, 2011.

• Compagno, Leonard, Marc Dando, and Sarah Fowler. *Sharks of the World.* Princeton, NJ: Princeton University Press, 2005.

• Cousteau, Jacques-Yves and Frédéric, Dumas. *The Silent World,* New York: Harper Collins, 1953

• Cousteau , Jacques-Yves, and Philippe Cousteau. *The Shark: Splendid Savage of the Sea.* Bookthrift Co., 1988.

• Cousteau , Jean-Michel. *Cousteau's Great White Shark.* New York: Harry N. Abrams, 1995.

• Cousteau , Jean-Michel, and Christine Causse. *Océans.* Paris: Delachaux et Niestlé, 2001.

• Ellis, Richard, and John E. McCosker, *Great White Shark,* Stanford University Press, 1995.

• Fallows, Chris. *Great White: The Majesty of Sharks.* San Francisco: Chronicle Books, 2009.

• Fox, Rodney. *Shark Man,* Norwood, South Australia: Omnibus Books, 2001

• Klimley, A. Peter and David G., Ainley. *Great White Sharks: The Biology of* Carcharodon carcharias. Maryland: Academic Press/Elsevier, 1996.

• Peschak, Thomas, and Michael Scholl, *South Africa's Great White Shark,* . Cape Town, South Africa: Struik Publishers, 2006.

• Trew Crist, Darlene, Gail Scowcroft, and James M. Harding Jr. *World Ocean Census: A Global Survey of Marine Life.* Buffalo, NY: Firefly Books, 2009.

FILMS

• *Blue Water, White Death,* MGM, 1971.

• *Expedition Great White,* National Geographic, 2010.

• *Great White Shark: Truth Behind the Legend,* National Geographic, 2000.

• *Great White Odyssey,* National Geographic, 2009.

• *Tracking White Sharks,* Abyss Productions, 2007.

INTERNET SITES

• SOS Great White
http://www.sosgrandblanc.com
http://www.patriceheraud.com (this site is dedicated to his work on the great white shark)

• IUCN Red List
http://www.iucnredlist.org

• Shark Alliance
http://www.sharkalliance.org

• Fox Shark Research Foundation
https://www.rodneyfox.com.au

• Marine Dynamics Shark Tours, André Hartman's company,
which specializes in cage diving:
http://sharkwatchsa.com

• Ocean Encounters (the expedition and cruise company operated by Frédéric Buyle, William Winram and Michèle Monico).
http://oceanencounters.net

• A site on the great white sharks of South Africa, created by Michael Scholl (not updated since 2007).
http://www.whitesharktrust.org

ACKNOWLEDGMENTS

I wish to extend my warmest gratitude to Dr. Charlie Huveneers (SARDI Aquatic Sciences, Australia) for his patience and his attentive re-reading of passages dedicated to scientific tagging programs conducted in South Australia. Thanks to the diver Frédéric Buyle for his observations and for the wonderful images of his diving near the Guadaloupe Island in Mexico. The interactions conducted by Catherine Vadon (MNHN) and Bernard Séret (MNHN/IRD) were incredible valuable to me, as well as the numerous documents and interpretations provided by the biologist Michael Scholl, Nicole's "discoverer." Another Nicole, Nicole Aussedat (Shark Alliance) helped me to better understand European regulations regarding finning.

I would also like to thank marine architect Jacques Rougerie, environmentalist Rémi Parmentier, and Phillippe Vallette, PDG of Nausicass. These three huge admirers of the Great Blue shared their preoccupations with all creatures that populate our seas, oceans—and our imaginations.

My thanks to Jacques-Yves Cousteau, who made me dream as a child, and to Maud Fontenoty, who gave us hope that future generations will live intelligently with the ocean, and maybe even with the great white.

Finally, I have deep emotional gratitude toward the photographer Patrice Héraud, without whom this writing adventure would not have been possible. Thanks Patrice, for your trust in this project and for your commitment. Lastly, thanks to Sandrine Stefaniak snf Éditions Glénat for their faith in this project.

Alexandrine Civard-Racinais

This book would not have seen the light of day if, on that fateful day of August 2000, I had not come to know Rodney and Andrew Fox. They must know that without them nothing would have been possible. Thanks to the crews of the two expedition vessels *FALIE* and *PRINCESS II* who, over 10 years, looked after us during rather hazardous crossings and during our deep-sea cage dives. Thanks to Jennifer Taylor, our Australian coordinator, for the passion she displays toward these marvelous animals to which she has devoted her entire life. Thanks to the crews of the Fox Shark Research Foundation, mainly to my friends, Dr. Rachel Robbins and Dr. Charlie Huveneers, for their advice over these many years.

Thanks to the members of my SOS Great White association, who contributed greatly to our tagging programs.

A warm thought, full of affection, goes out to the children of the Flora-Tristan de Martignas-sur-Jalle School (33) for their support and their involvement during the 2010 expedition. Thanks to their teachers who allowed them to be patrons to our two great white sharks, Biscotto and Paillette.

Finally, thanks to Sandine Stefaniak and to Editions Glénat for having believed in this project and for allowing me to bring it to its conclusion.

Patrice Héraud

1667